It seems redundant to state that Frankie Boyle is a writer at the start of a book that he has written. His Wikipedia page no longer refers to him as 'pessimistic' and he hopes that you, in your own life, one day experience this searing level of vindication. The mundane details of Frankie Boyle are available elsewhere. Let us instead note that he is currently doing a lot of yoga; has a laissez-faire parenting style; is very happy with his recent purchase of a massage gun; and his next holiday will be in Greece.

D0810079

THE FUTURE OF BRITISH POLITICS

Frankie Boyle

unbound

First published in 2020

Unbound
Level 1, Devonshire House, One Mayfair Place, London W1J 8AJ
www.unbound.com

With the kind permission of Tortoise Media

Text design by Ellipsis, Glasgow

A CIP record for this book is available from the British Library

ISBN 978-1-80018-010-9 (paperback)
ISBN 978-1-80018-015-4 (ebook)

Printed in Great Britain by CPI Group (UK)

3 5 7 9 8 6 4

FOREWORD

Where and who do we want to be?

How might we get there?

What might happen if we stay on our current course?

This is one of the five books that, together, comprise the first set of FUTURES essays. Each short book in the set presents a beautifully written, original future vision by an accomplished writer and subject expert. Read individually, we hope these essays will inform, entertain and challenge. Together, we hope they will inspire readers to imagine what might lie ahead, to figure out how they might like the future to look, and think about how, collectively, we might make the transition from here to there, from now to then.

Over the life of the series we aim to publish a diverse range of voices, covering as broad a view of the future as possible. We ask our authors to write in a spirit of pragmatic hope, and with a commitment to map out potential future landscapes, highlighting both beauties and dangers. We are hugely proud of each of the essays individually, and of the set overall. We hope you get as much out of reading – and arguing with – them as we have from the process of getting them out into the world.

This first set of FUTURES would have been impossible to publish without the enthusiastic support of Tortoise Media, Unbound and the subscribers whose names you'll find listed at the back of each essay. Michael Kowalski, Tortoise's Head of Product, introduced co-founder Katie Vanneck-Smith to the idea, and she made it happen. Annabel Shepherd-Barron's unparalleled strategic capabilities kept the project steady and on course. Matthew d'Ancona offered superb editorial guidance with extraordinary kindness and generosity of spirit, and Jon Hill's designs for the book jackets are elegant perfection. Fiona Lensvelt, DeAndra Lupu and their colleagues at Unbound have proved wonderfully creative and flexible throughout.

This first set of FUTURES essays was commissioned in autumn 2019, in the midst of the Brexit saga, and edited in spring 2020, in lockdown, as Covid-19 changed everything. As we write, it looks unlikely that, by the time you read this, our lives will have settled into any kind of normal – old or new. Still, argument, wit and enlightened thought remain amongst our greatest strengths as a species, and even during an era as stressful and disorienting as the one we are experiencing, imagination, hope and compassion can help us mine greater reserves of resilience than we might expect. We hope these essays can, in a small way, help us find some light at the end of the tunnel.

Professor Max Saunders, Series Editor
Dr Lisa Gee, Programme Director and Editor
May 2020

INTRODUCTION

I finished this essay just before coronavirus came along and rendered it all as relevant to the zeitgeist as *The Diary of Samuel Pepys*. I've left the text as it was submitted in late February 2020, as I think it's instructive to see my breezy attempts to wish away the looming disaster; probably one of the few times I've been in tune with the national mood. The year 2020 began with Australia on fire and a billion animals dead – it's sobering to think that will now be the feel-good story of the year. Remember at the beginning of the year when Rod Stewart lamped a security guard and Justin Bieber announced that he had Lyme disease? Dizzying times; it genuinely felt like the world was a wonderful place to be. For many of you, it will have been surprising to learn what was expected of you during an Apocalypse. You always wondered whether you would be fleeing; fortifying a bunker; or camping on a motorway roundabout. Turns out you're working from home. Trying to get a spreadsheet about body bags finished before the provisional deadline of your own death.

Mistakes have been made in the handling of the crisis. Like flying the Buckingham Palace flag at half-mast when the Queen's not in, which is just an advert for burglars. In my local park, someone has tried to cheer people up by chalking 'You Got This!' on the ground. Literally the last thing you want to hear in a pandemic. There have also been a variety of embarrassing attempts by famous people to boost morale. If celebrities want to keep our spirits up, they should accept that what would raise those spirits the most is to see a couple of them really lose it big time. We've all developed our little coping strategies. One easy way to completely remove the urge to visit your family is simply to put up Christmas decorations.

Glaswegian men have found it trickier to stay two metres apart than most, what with so many unable to keep even a hundred away from an ex. Here, news of a pandemic seemed to energise the elderly: the streets were full of people who normally only leave their homes to vote for fascism. Before the lockdown, old people in Glasgow, apparently determined to flood the housing market with cheap bungalows, looked like they had formed a search party to go and find the coronavirus. It was sinister just to catch sight of an old person in the distance, much like the feeling you get when you see an antelope in a nature documentary and know it's not going to end well. I'm sure we all know fatalists from the older generation who are saying things like, 'If I get it, I get it. There's no point trying to avoid it.' Some of these people lived through the Blitz, and were presumably mental back then as well. While everyone was hunkered down in Anderson shelters in the dead of night listening to the Luftwaffe passing overhead, your grandad was probably up on the roof testing his Christmas lights.

What have we learned so far? Well, maybe best not to vote for people who think of you as a 'herd'. The government's response to the crisis reminds me, more than anything, of that bit in *Apocalypse Now* when Kurtz asks, 'Are my methods unsound?' and Willard replies, 'I don't see any method at all, sir.' In early briefings Boris Johnson would pull a concerned face, to show that he is a serious person. Unfortunately, the face he pulls when he tries to look like a serious person is the sort of face that an actual serious person pulls to show that they are confused. In many ways, if the whole cabinet are killed by a virus just after their election victory, it will pretty much be the ending of *The War of the Worlds*. The designated survivor, Dominic Raab, who seems to instantaneously develop every symptom of the disease whenever he's asked to read out a press release, looks like the very man to lead us right over the lip of the volcano.

We will soon get back to full employment. As the government's lack of planning means anyone tested negative can spend ten-hour shifts blowing into the mouths of the infected as a human respirator. We're seeing exhibition centres in London, Manchester, Birmingham and Glasgow converted into temporary hospitals and morgues. Which has a certain logic: if you've ever been to watch a band at one, you'll know they're among the most sterile places in the UK. For many who don't get a call back from Tesco, there awaits a summer job bagging cadavers, and at the end of the shift being charged six quid for a short-measured pint of flat Carlsberg served in a plastic tumbler. We should be affording the NHS staff and patients a level of dignity in these worrying times. It's distressing enough to be told that you're being put on a ventilator; we shouldn't be adding to that by having the news broken by a doctor wearing a Spider-Man mask and boxing gloves.

Toby Young questioned whether there was an economic case for preserving the lives of the elderly and vulnerable, and at least showed a certain honesty by politically aligning himself with a deadly virus. There's still a question mark over whether any virus would want to be associated with Toby Young, and at the time of writing both Ebola and AIDS have sought to distance themselves from his remarks. When Toby Young pops up on my TV, I can't be the only person in the country who involuntarily coughs at the screen. Of course this villainous kneecap is so hated by everyone in the country that he's the only man who hasn't seen his lifestyle change since social distancing was introduced. At least now when people cross the road when they see him, he can pretend there's a more upbeat reason. Toby Young has always embodied contradictions, even if simply by being interested in eugenics while looking like an unviable foetus. In this case you have to wonder how he can be against trashing the economy for the sake of people who have a year or two left to live, while still supporting Brexit.

I had that stress dream last night. Where I volunteered to battle the virus face to face. But halfway through the cleaner pulls out the plug on the shrink ray so she can use her Henry Hoover, and I'm left living in a fluff-filled matchbox, having to bathe in a thimble and go to work on a galloping mouse. Perhaps the prospect of meeting your end in an epidemic is different when you have comprehensively fucked your own life up; part of me thinks that if I die now, I can call this thing a draw.

The whole crisis does raise some interesting questions though: if we all agree that we can't have the weakest people in society dying as a healthcare system, then why do we tolerate it as an economic system? We see articles about people who have stockpiled hand sanitiser to sell at a markup, but they are the people the system we live in supports, and that is what speculation is. How do we ever find a way out of this within our current system? Drugs need to be developed in the public sector: Big Pharma has no interest in putting itself out of business by creating universal vaccines, and spends more on advertising than research.

Indeed, you have to wonder if the virus is so very different from extractive capitalism. It commandeers the manufacturing elements of its hosts, gets them to make stuff for it, kills a fair few, but not enough to stop it spreading. There is no normal for us to go back to. People sleeping in the streets wasn't normal; children living in poverty wasn't normal; neither was our taxes helping to bomb the people of Yemen. Using other people's lives to pile up objects wasn't normal; the whole thing was absurd. Governments are currently busy pouring money into propping up existing inequalities, and bailing out businesses that have made their shareholders rich. The world's worst people think that everybody is going to come out of this in a few months and go willingly back into a kind of numbing servitude. Surely it's time to start imagining something better.

THE FUTURE OF
BRITISH POLITICS

In this essay I have aimed for something approaching optimism, despite the fact that it was written during a Scottish winter so bleak that I found myself imagining my own funeral. 'Partner. Father. Friend. Confidant. Boss. Colleague... Frankie really did kill a lot of people.' I know people say that not washing means you're depressed, but I'm not sure that having four baths a day is an amazing sign either. Yet, having thought about it for a while, there is a limited case for optimism about Britain's future. The coronavirus, for example, will never really spread here as the British are experts at avoiding human contact. We may be criticised for being a nation of iPod-wearing, card-swiping sociophobes whose sex lives are conducted by Insta and text, but at least we're not going to die of a cough before our ultimate descent into suicide. Really, I only wrote that to get into the feel of the sweeping, baseless predictions that will characterise much of this essay. Let's be honest: by the time you read this, anything could have happened here with coronavirus. We lose a couple dozen people every time it snows. To really understand Britain's future we will, counter-intuitively, have to take a very long look at its past, because that is where the attitudes and expectations that will shape the future have been formed. Indeed, our lack of knowledge about our history has made it difficult to understand even the present moment. For example, it's impossible to fully understand what's happening in Hong Kong right now without knowing that Britain acquired the territory after forcing China to get hooked on opium, and that it's the geopolitical equivalent of a junkie's bike.

The section of any large bookshop that deals with British history is always a bracing reminder of the true relationship between the British public and their founding myths. There's normally a wall devoted almost entirely to the glory days of Empire, and you'll have to look hard for alternative or radical takes. Fittingly, I suppose, those little acts of rebellion are overwhelmed by the massed ranks of conformity: fat mainstream paperbacks; luxurious-looking hardbacks; and prestigious TV tie-ins. Standard bestsellers on Empire, no doubt in the interests of jollying things along, tend to minimise the various famines and drug wars that were so key to imperial development, while Churchill is the subject of many an amusing elision. In this context, you can understand how the British people can see something like the Raj (estimates range from ten million excess deaths right up to thirty-five million) as a feasible backdrop for romantic period dramas. Which is not really so terribly different from Germany producing Holocaust rom-coms. So perhaps it is time for an evaluation of the role that Empire plays in British identity, because I like to think that, as we were watching the German version of Hugh Grant spell out a marriage proposal in bodies or whatever, we might reflect that they were labouring under some fairly major delusions about their place in history.

It's not simply an academic issue. A country, if Britain even is a country, that doesn't understand its history is going to be unable to comprehend its obligations. You can see this in Britain's attitude to refugees. 'Why don't these people stop thinking about money and stop at the nearest country?' ask people who drive around looking for cheap petrol. Comments on refugee stories in the *Daily Mail* are usually along the lines of 'Stay where you are and sort your own country out', from readers who haven't voted since *Bake Off* got moved to Channel 4. (I always feel safe criticising the *Daily Mail*. Only a handful of their readers know who I am, and even then only because their grandchildren left the TV on BBC2 during visiting hours.) Of course, one of the main motivators for refugees coming to Britain is that they speak

English. Which brings us to the rather awkward business of why they speak English. It's the same reason that I speak English, my parents having moved to Scotland from the imperial punchbag of Ireland. The reason that anyone you meet in Ireland today is ridiculously, gratingly cheerful is that the only people who stayed after about 1842 were hopeless optimists.

They say that the sun never set on the British Empire. I mean it did, but it was hard to see behind the huge pile of dead Indians. It is argued that the Empire helped many countries by opening up trade markets. And at the end of the day, isn't that what life is all about? Okay, yes, your wife has been bludgeoned to death and your children have been forced into indentured servitude but at least someone in Hull wants to buy your mango. It's easy to forget that the Empire viewed itself as being about trade, although in practice this was a euphemism for exploitation (sometimes this is quite explicit: the East India Company started as a trading concern but quickly made most of its profits from onerous land taxes, often collected through torture). The argument of Brexit is in some ways a sublimated, and quite correct, recognition that Britain's relationship with the EU is actually about trade, and doesn't offer it opportunities for exploitation. Because of the Empire, we developed an elite class addicted to enormous returns on investment, only possible through constant growth. As this becomes impossible, Brexit happens so profits can be delivered through cannibalising previously protected resources, including people.

It is amazing to consider that we ever had an empire. We struggle to organise a weekly bin collection literally in our own backyards and yet we thought we could do better four thousand miles away, in 45-degree heat, in another language. In Victorian times the rule of thumb for wealthy families was that the oldest son would run the estate in Britain, and the second son would travel to the colonies to find his fortune. Looked at that way it's easy to see imperial excess as nothing more than the symptoms of second-child syndrome; when Hugo hears that his brother back home has got the orangery up and running, it is in many ways a natural response to systematically starve twenty million people.

There are only fourteen Overseas Territories remaining, one of them being Gibraltar. I guess after centuries of plundering the world all you really want to do is kick back and have a fry up on a hill that stinks of monkey shit. Currently the British Empire consists of only 250,000 people. Pitcairn Island is home to fifty of them. Pitcairn was initially colonised by mutineers from the *Bounty* and a handful of Tahitians. Sounds like paradise. Until you discover that in 2004 seven men – a third of the male population – were convicted of underage sex crimes. You can understand why the British elite are so keen to hold onto this beauty. A third of the men being sex criminals creates a sense of nostalgia, reminding our Establishment of prep school, university, Westminster, and any time they're in a car with two other people.

If you grow up in a racist society, you have to guard against the racism that will subconsciously become part of you. If modern British identity is constructed by its history of imperialism, then where can we see it? Obviously we see it in the fawning news items when the royals go abroad and receive traditional native welcomes (perhaps they should occasionally reciprocate with a traditional British arrival, running up the beach with rifles and giving everybody syphilis), but do we see it in the Commonwealth Games? We hear it when Boris Johnson, a sort of semi-sentient candy floss, talks of 'piccaninnies' with 'watermelon smiles', or when Jeremy Clarkson jokes about 'slopes' and lazy Irishmen, but do we hear it when visiting English comedians at the Edinburgh Festival drawl about 'the Scotch' and their love of shortbread and offal? Did you recognise it in my joke about the Irish being gratingly cheerful? Aren't they all equally the kind of things that could have been heard in the mess hall of any colonial outpost? One of the privileges of whiteness is being able to see racists as entirely laughable (indeed, it's hard to think of anything more laughable than people who suffer from inbreeding moaning about diversity), because for us racism is always abstract.

Britain's disengagement from its history isn't just a problem for the right. Many Labour supporters' reaction to the party's anti-Semitism problems was to insist that they were historically the party of anti-racism. This is wildly ahistorical: Attlee's government referred to the arrival of the *Empire Windrush* as 'an incursion' and presided over a brutal Malayan war (ironically to protect British profits from a growing left and union movement). Blair launched a racist war on Iraq in living memory. The fact that Labour, even when under its historically most anti-racist leader, could only celebrate the achievements of its past and not acknowledge the crimes is itself an echo of imperial attitudes. For imperial politicians, the past was just a place you visited to mine propaganda, and they would find our modern political discourse very familiar.

Another ripple of Empire can be seen in the way in Britain we can easily slip into the imperial mindset of the unearned moral high ground: there's nothing more inherently colonial than the idea that you and your friends are some of the only good people in the world. Left-wing liberals (like me, to be honest) are often blind to their own ideology in the same way that they perceive middle-class people speaking English as not having an accent. Sometimes the colonial attitudes are obvious, such as when politicians propose British military interventions in faraway civil wars. Or when new-school atheists denounce Islam as barbarism, or compare it unfavourably with Christianity. Indeed, I'm often surprised at how relaxed some of the British left is about rich white men telling people dying in rubble that they don't need God.

One subtler strand of imperial hangover in British liberal thought is the prevalence of the idea that good and bad are self-evident, often summarised into some version of 'just don't be a dick'. The idea that it is possible in our society to live a purely moral life, that it is even simple to do so, is, I think, a profound misreading, informed by colonial certainties. It's also pretty close to the slogan of Google, in case you were wondering how much of a dick you were being. These unearned feelings of moral superiority are insidious. The other day I found myself expressing disappointment that Dead Prez had allowed their music to be used in an advert. Dead Prez, finally getting paid for their genre-defining politicised hip-hop, were the villains in this story, and I was the hero who had bravely, over a period of many years, pirated their music.

I think this mindset comes in part from a misconception that the Empire represented some kind of moral journey: that it begins in slavery and conquest and ends in reconciliation and Commonwealth. Slavery was abolished against a background of slave rebellions and increasing industrialisation. As so often happens, a moral course was found to be possible only once the business got difficult. Much in the way that Hollywood sex cases have found themselves on trial now that cinema has been replaced by YouTube videos of people unboxing blenders. The only true reconciliation the Empire cared about was with the slave owners, who were fully compensated.

People ask whether the class system is still relevant in the United Kingdom, and perhaps the word 'Kingdom' gives us some kind of clue. It certainly affects how we express ourselves if we wish to be taken seriously. I mean even this is written in a very different register from the phonetic, demotic Scottish I might use online. The kind of satire that gets published in Britain tends to echo stylistically, more than anything, P. G. Wodehouse, and is almost entirely Horatian in tone. I do wonder sometimes if the predominance of the Horatian, elliptical tone in British satire doesn't come from the fact that it makes sense for a society that is so obviously in the wrong to think that the truth is best told in a very roundabout way.

A study in 2014 concluded that 59 per cent of British people thought that the Empire was more something to be proud than ashamed of. This is a result that has been striven for by the British state, which staged Operation Legacy during decolonisation to physically destroy records of the crimes committed under British rule. The acute lack of representation in our culture should be looked on as a continuation of this mindset. Look at directing, the position that has a unique position in our cultural psyche as a discipline demanding cerebral and artistic insight. Just 1.5 per cent of film and television directors in Britain are black or minority ethnic, roughly one-sixth of what it should be. I mean, we do discuss representation occasionally in the British mainstream, but we rarely proceed to the obvious and awkward conclusion. That non-white people are viewed, in this culture, as lacking qualities both of intelligence and artistic impulse. That non-white people are viewed in our culture as less than human, by a society that they are expected to live in. This is a delusion that Britain embraces willingly, as it fears their stories, possibly because they might include an awkward section where we blew their granny out of a cannon. Non-representation is just the cultural equivalent of not being able to meet someone's gaze.

So let's look at the future, but with the caveat that everything about our current situation is a product of our imperial past, and that if Britain doesn't come to understand its own history it is doomed.

If we're to look at what the future might be for British politics, let's start by addressing a couple of things that could mean all other calculations are irrelevant. Climate catastrophe, and apocalyptic technological changes, could well make everything else I write about here not so much a footnote in history as one of those stray pubes you occasionally come across when turning a page. I'm going to get them out of the way now because extinction-level events are actually something of a whimsical mood lightener when viewed between colonial history and the likely direction of Westminster politics.

I find that the climate crisis is the hardest subject for live comedy, perhaps because people are just trying to shut it out. Sometimes we simply deny the truth because it's easier not to think about it. As with Britain's role in Yemen, where we're involved in a proxy war that we don't see ourselves being involved in. In much the same way that Peter Sutcliffe may have just seen himself as a hammer tester. This year scientists reported a record 18 degrees in the Arctic. Which is particularly shocking to people from Glasgow because we've sunbathed in colder temperatures than that. I think it's good that we call young people now Generation Z, as if admitting that it's pretty much all over. I'm not a total pessimist: I think that even after a nuclear war, human civilisation will probably live on, in the stories of super-advanced cockroaches trying to work out where they got cancer from. Treating the planet like a front garden on the way home from the chippie means that, before long, a continuous floating mat of plastic will even rob us of the simple final pleasure of being able to walk into the sea.

We can expect hotter summers and wetter winters. The great thing about roasting-hot summers is that Britain will be sexually-transmitted-disease-free, as the population will effectively be pasteurised. When Australia burned in 2019–20 the world cared because of the beautiful landscapes and animals that were so badly affected. Britain is not going to be in the same position. No one is going to give a shit when our news broadcasts a melting bus stop and a pigeon coughing. The overwhelming reaction from the rest of the planet will be subdued amusement. In fact, there will be people actively encouraging fires, if only to clear out Essex and turn it into the kangaroo sanctuary the world so badly needs.

Even though the climate crisis will disproportionately affect the developing world, British climate protests often carelessly erase the struggles of activists in other countries who are on the front line of the looming catastrophe. While they are well intentioned, there is something alienating about the predominantly white and middle-class British climate movement, and something in the way they imagine polite protest will achieve something that denies all we know of the British state. It's dispiriting to see people who believe anything can be achieved by being polite to the police, and the general air of 'I dare say the PLO would have gotten a bit further, if only they'd shown some manners.' Despite this, I actually think Prince Charles is well suited to being a leading environmentalist. Partly because he's spent his career being routinely ignored, and also because the royals have done their bit to shorten car journeys, one in particular springing to mind.

I predict that, primed by decades of misinformation, the British will react badly to any major action demanded to decarbonise the economy. Which is sad, because action on climate could actually be good for the national mood. Any restrictions on flights will mean it's back to the glory days of holidays here in the UK: a week or two of picking sand out of candy floss before squeezing into a hotel lift with a screeching hen party pressing the buttons with an oversized dildo. Or walking into a pub, hearing everyone start talking in Welsh, and thinking, 'These people must really hate me, this is Stratford.' Still, I've done my bit to reduce emissions. One short evening class in ventriloquism and I can stop pretty much any cremation. I won't be cremated myself. I plan to have my body frozen in liquid nitrogen then placed on a plinth, so it can be shattered like a windscreen with a high C delivered by an opera singer, largely because I've always wanted to leave this world to the sound of someone screaming, 'Quick! Cover the vol-au-vents!'

Mark Fisher, the cultural theorist whose 2017 suicide seems increasingly prescient, coined the term 'capitalist realism' to describe the way that we could imagine the end of the world more easily than we could imagine the end of capitalism. I think that has gone now, and that people can, increasingly, imagine a future shaped by something other than capitalism. Perhaps the system itself is even admitting its decrepitude metaphorically, by delivering a US presidential race between two candidates apparently suffering from dementia. I think of what we inhabit now as more of a consumer realism. We believe that we can refine or replace capitalism with something that still delivers all the stuff. And so there are people who passionately engage with the climate crisis, but still take flights. I suppose our hopes for the survival of the earth seem to rest, as much as anything, on our ability to imagine a different way of living.

I've always been excited by technology: maybe it's the end of that last Bill Hicks show I loved, but I've always felt that the universe meant us to explore the stars, and this is the reason that it made all of the people on earth so awful. Despite our advances, the most obvious technological threat to humanity is still old-school nuclear oblivion. In the event of a nuclear attack there will be a three-minute warning. But everything will work out because if, at the moment that warning sounds, you can take enough acid, those three minutes will last for about sixty thousand years. The white light of the explosion will creep towards you very gradually over the centuries, like an ice sheet. The missiles will hang in the sky like the moon. Over the years, a white-hot bus will gradually inch its way through the front of your conservatory, your dead neighbour strapped to the front like Garfield on a bin lorry. Many of your later years will be spent at quite a high altitude, watching your body gradually disassemble. When your organs start to leave, you will have time to wish them goodbye. You will say farewell to your penis like a first-born son who is going off to university. You'll wonder if there's a tear in your eye, but it will just be the fact that your eye itself is boiling.

A more mundane threat is the sociopathy of giant Silicon Valley corporations. What can we learn from their rise? Possibly that Hitler might have just about made it if only he'd fitted out the Reichstag with a ping-pong table and some hammocks. If tech giants effectively become the new governments, it's fair to assume they'll want armies. Conventional war reporting will no longer make sense when the social media firms deploy armies: 'These casualty figures are off the scale, but the photos from the front – everyone just looks like they're having a great time!' Of course, the Internet was invented by a Brit. What other nation would want to take racism to a previously unimaginable format? There are upsides: it tackles loneliness. After a few hours on social media you think, 'Thank fuck I'm alone.' My gran has never surfed the Internet. I thought it might be because she's scared of big data or fraud; turns out she doesn't want to stumble across any of the porn she made in the thirties. Why do old people find technology so difficult to adopt? Although you could turn that round and say what is it that the younger generation find so difficult about buying their trousers from the back of a Sunday newspaper magazine?

Getting sense out of social media is like trying to tune an AM radio under Niagara Falls. Many men online display a curious mix of misogyny and old-school chivalry: you can picture them dispensing a courteous 'after you, my dear' as they hold open the hatch to their basement.

One disturbing aspect of new media is the explosion of conspiracism; a denialism that borders on a new kind of epistemology. With that kind of radical doubt, it's confusing that they ever manage to privilege one source of information over another. Yet they do, and we end up with anti-vaxxers who worry about being poisoned by corporations while spending all their time on Facebook. One of the world's foremost authorities on AI has hypothesised that AI algorithms, in their quest to target advertising, have exhausted all other factors and may have begun to try to make their audiences more predictable. In this theory, polarising content is directed towards users because once they're in a MAGA hat or foaming about 'anti-Semitism smears', their behaviour is easier to anticipate and easier to target advertising to. It's an unsettling premise, and we have to wonder where such a thing would end. Genuine predictability is only available in totalitarian societies.

We shouldn't worry about Huawei; the Western tech companies that dominate our lives are far more dangerous. Admittedly, I might only be saying that as I have a highly specific fetish where I'm only able to successfully masturbate while being watched by President Xi's Politburo. If we can get that up and running via 5G it would certainly be welcomed by the Asian actors I have currently cast (ask me to get behind a scheme promoting non-white stage talent and I really go for it). I say get Huawei in. If there's one thing that's going to spice up masturbation it's knowing that a bunch of workers in the Forbidden City are clustered round a monitor watching, and that at least one of them will go home that evening and do the same thing thinking about what they saw, while being watched by their line manager via a camera in a ceiling tile, who's also masturbating. And being watched by his superior through a fibre-optic tube the width of a human hair concealed in a Hello Kitty cushion. And as I ejaculate I'll lock eyes with my smartphone and shriek in perfect Cantonese – 'I bet you never predicted this did you, Nostra-fuckin-damus!'

With the extent of London's CCTV, the annual marathon could become the replacement organ equivalent of a lobster tank in a fish restaurant: oligarchs paying a subscription, a camera turning slowly on a lamp post as Vladimir Putin picks out a spare kidney.

'That one! He's got a certain spring in his step.'

'I'm not totally comfortable with this, sir.'

'It's only a costume, we won't be killing a real rhino!'

(I enjoy watching the London Marathon because I see it as the one day when the capital's trafficked sex workers stand a real chance of making a break for freedom... a crowd big enough to disappear into, their bleakly battle-hardened knees propelling them to escape velocity.)

Personally, I'm crossing my fingers for the invention of consciousness transfer. Largely so that I can find someone diplomatic, well-mannered and debonair to annually take charge of my body for a month to redeem the unspeakability of my past year's behaviour, while I spend a much-needed break as a tortoise. Indeed, advances in tech will be driven by our increasing insecurities. By 2050 a simulacrum of us could be out there, a holographic better self, strutting about purposefully to enhance our perceived status, the real 'us' paying for it with meagre income from jobs as GM-modified man crops, the glucose produced by our new-found ability to photosynthesise squeezed hourly from our multi-teats. 'Just another eight years,' we'll think, as we search for the software update needed to ensure fake 'us' knows exactly which holographic cutlery to reach for when dining with other holograms further up the virtual social hierarchy. When it's time to retire, the years sprawled out in the furious midday sun will have taken their toll, tumours sprouting from our back like bobbles on a cashmere jumper. Maybe this technology will exist soon, but it's not here yet. Or so my afternoon of trying to out these projected monstrosities by thrusting my hand through strangers' torsos would suggest.

The much-ballyhooed Internet of Things (what is a smart bin? In my day that was a dog) will see a surge in demand for rare metals, forcing up their price. Combine that with the invention of the brain-computer interface and there will be times when the spare capacity of human consciousness will be a cheaper option for processing and storage. For a nutritious bowl of soup we'll be plugged in, with a thousand others, running algorithms to more precisely push a new wonder mop to lonely housewives idly googling through a Valium comedown. Until new sources of these essential elements are found we'll be able to clear head space in order to offer a handful of terabytes of storage, spending our working day weeping, not just at how we've lost all but a silhouette awareness of that magical week in Aberystwyth, but because as our brain scrolls through a lifetime of other people's stored images we watch a thousand unknown babies grow, wither, then die. Well, this whole section actually hasn't turned out to be as upbeat as I'd hoped. Let's move on.

And so to the mundane reality of what we can reasonably predict about the future direction of the British political system. Again, some understanding of the history of what we're talking about is useful. The Conservative Party represents the interests of capital. In the Victorian period, *Capital* was a book by Karl Marx which explained that our way of life couldn't continue. Today, Capital is a radio station where my daughter listens to Ed Sheeran songs interspersed with adverts for dog food, but in many ways the message remains the same. Tories are there to represent the interests of capital to the electorate. The interests of capital are completely at odds with those of the electorate, so conservatism is alive with internal contradictions. There's obviously a disconnect between avoiding inheritance tax and trashing the environment, for example. Equally, the Tories will have to combine pandering to anti-migrant hostility with the fact our economy's fucked without them. No doubt Boris Johnson will find an elegant compromise. Perhaps having migrant workers spend the nights bobbing in the shallows, so they can shuffle up our beaches each morning before changing into dry work clothes that they keep buried among the dunes.

The Conservative Party is built on the fault lines of contradiction. Their own cabinet is a clear indictment of the way that inherited wealth fundamentally undermines natural selection. These are people who tell you the arts don't matter but spend a significant chunk of their income sending their children to schools with theatres, libraries and orchestras. They'll tell you that the places the Empire invaded had no culture, and yet insist that our museums remain full of their stuff. The contradictions of our society are managed by having an elite class who have internalised them, often through attending public school and Oxbridge (Oxbridge is a compound term formed from the words obnoxious and privilege). What we often think of as the self-belief instilled by an elite education is really a kind of class exceptionalism, a belief that privilege is earned through talent and hard work, against all of the available evidence. If you doubt this, simply ask the most left-wing Oxbridge graduate you can find what role they think their background played in their success.

One of the problems with left-wing discourse in Britain is that it seeks to moralise its opponents without ever considering what they really think. A corollary of having a Conservative Party dedicated to misrepresenting the world to its own electoral base is that they try not to be honest in public. So if you're trying to shame them about something like inequality, you should be aware that many of them think inequality is a good thing, that it provides strivers with both incentive and example. Moralising with such people is like giving your cancer a good telling off.

In Brexit negotiations, the Tories will no doubt stage a big row with the EU, and try to manufacture some general sense of brinkmanship, but some kind of high alignment deal with a few carveouts seems most likely. The UK seems keen to reach a Canada-style arrangement with the EU. Which means they are legally bound to take any of the royal family that we break. Part of the Brexit narrative has been that we need to become the Britain we once were: a nation at sea, where the sun never sets. Both of which will be achieved, but only because of climate change. Part of the early negotiations has involved Britain trying to keep European fleets out of British waters, as due to flooding British waters now often extend as far inland as Derbyshire. The great thing about climate change for the Europeans is they can forget about fish, sail right into the Yorkshire Dales and fill their holds with lamb.

Brexit may actually transpire to have done the country a great service by keeping one of the most incompetent cabinets in history away from doing any actual governing. I'm still struggling to work out whether Boris Johnson represents the interface of the public school system and foetal alcohol syndrome, or what happens when Pixar is infiltrated by the last surviving Nazi war criminal. The majority of Tory MPs would rather have no deal than still work under the European Court of Justice. This is because they grew up with safety nets: they don't need the rule of law because someone will always bail them out. So they live a life of risks, whether it be waiting for Daddy to die before next term's fees are due, or hoping that what the Filipino nanny is screaming is that she enjoys BDSM.

In South Wales racist attacks went up 77 per cent after the referendum vote. I'm not certain whether to be appalled at their racism or admire that they managed to keep such a tsunami of hatred inside until they thought it was allowed. The fact that people from South Wales can suppress high levels of hatred towards their fellow man is what makes them such naturals to work in call centres. Of course, the racism debate is more serious and complex than that. Might a squeeze on legal migrant labour mean more people being brought here illegally? I'm not certain people traffickers will be fazed by one more border, much as I don't think it was a bad day at work if Harold Shipman wandered upstairs to find a twin. Even if we have a disastrous No Deal exit, Leave supporters aren't going to blame themselves. They're going to blame the same people they always blame: foreigners, people on benefits and the guy next door who won't cut back his conifers. Nonetheless, you can see why some people are worried that aspects of our national character won't survive Brexit. Is it even possible to queue and loot at the same time?

Still, many Remain supporters have shown themselves to be hopelessly middle class. Complaining about what was written on the outside of a bus, while the inside contains the sweltering, noise-polluted, working poor having to travel an extra stop for affordable clothes since you decided an organic pizzeria would be a quirky addition to their local market, shows that you are just as much an architect of this divide as a lying algorithm.

The EU is inherently racist – it's a gathering of white nations specifically halting at the line where a tan becomes permanent. I mean, in many ways it's quite a feat for Britain's racists to reject this historically racist institution for being full of foreigners. I suppose I think that Britain flatters itself a little with ideas of being different from the EU. They're run by slightly different types of elites, but for a long time now everyone's interests have been the same: making money for bastards in the hope that one day they become the bastard that someone has to make money for.

Boris Johnson, an evolutionary dead end of the Honey Monster, has made the steampunk suggestion of building a bridge across the sea to Northern Ireland. Of course, the plan has been unhelpfully undermined by so-called experts, who fail to understand that an impossible structure built in high winds across a million tonnes of decommissioned explosives might well be the metaphor Brexit needs. Personally, I think this crazed Tower of Babel-style project might be the ideal thing to distract us from reality. Soon Britain will look around the slag heap on which it has thrown itself, and there will no doubt be an atmosphere of recrimination: upbeat talk of bridges between countries, underground cities or possibly a pneumatic moon-tube might be all that stands between us and chaos. At least the bridge shows that Boris is clearly thinking about need post-withdrawal – hugely improved suicide facilities, the death toll doubling as jumpers sink the rafts of all those still strong enough to paddle to Ireland.

Yet who is to say that Britain won't solve the problems created by Brexit the same way they've always done, through technological innovation? Perhaps our top scientists are already hard at work inventing a sauce that makes your pets taste better. I can't help being reminded of the Edward Snowden revelations when the head of the Cabinet Office went round to the *Guardian*'s offices and wanted them to smash their hard drives with a hammer, because he didn't really understand what data was. Similarly, we might not have a modern understanding of what sovereignty is. Perhaps a modern concept of sovereignty might involve owning the property in your capital city, or your own railway system. At the moment Britain is in a strange position where we seem to be sanguine about foreigners owning our infrastructure, but we just don't want them picking our fruit.

At this point it's maybe worth reflecting on the sort of people who will make up the government, especially as it's likely to last for a decade. Being in cabinet meetings at the moment must be like sharing a railway carriage with a medical school revue on their way to the Edinburgh Festival. Dominic Raab began his career as an international lawyer, I like to imagine this was probably because anyone with English as their first language could tell what a useless cunt he is; while Matt Hancock looks like he's still in the friendzone with his own wife. The actual Home Secretary Priti Patel is surely not allowed to use her gas hob without supervision. MI5 have denied claims that they've withheld intelligence from the Home Secretary. If anyone is guilty of that, it's God.

The members of our elites who used to go into politics now choose real power by going into the finance sector. And we are left with people like Michael Gove. It seems unfair we have to endure Michael Gove, just because a chance knock from a meter reader spared him the mercy of the midwife's pillow. A man who somehow stands out even on a Tory front bench that looks like the final few paragraphs of some particularly bracing H. P. Lovecraft. Michael Gove, a man who is leaving his body to science fiction. Michael Gove, who looks like a witch tried to turn a schoolboy into a snail and forgot the words halfway through. Michael Gove, who looks like what remains after the third horse of the apocalypse snags its cock on a fence. Michael Gove – brought to life in 1986 when a mascot for an Oxford *University Challenge* team was struck by lightning. It's not that he doesn't have any human qualities – he does, that's the tragedy. Michael Gove is human, certainly, but he is not how we like to think of ourselves. There are no movies where the hero is like Michael Gove. In fact, the only echo of Michael Gove in the entirety of the Western canon would be an occasional supporting character in a cautionary fable for children. A shepherd boy who spread rumours about the sinister ways of the people from the next village, only to find they were reluctant to help him when he was carried off by a pederast.

Many Conservative politicians are little more than a collection of personality defects developed in an attempt to lure their father out from behind the *Daily Telegraph* during the six days a year they weren't using the top bunk at school as the forced sodomy equivalent of a life raft during a shark attack. I also have a theory that Tory men find out they're into autoerotic asphyxiation after they attempt domestic tasks unsupervised and end up boil-washing a polo-necked jumper.

One of the reasons evil people triumph is that good people have much fuller diaries. So when the fun people are getting asked to do stuff, and go to barbecues, our future rulers are left standing round in little clumps of mediocrity thinking about how they can privatise the health service. And that's why it all gets formalised into university societies and private members' clubs and stuff: they just don't know how to have a proper friendship. They're sitting there once the small talk dies down whispering, 'What do we do now? Fuck a pig?'

I still think Boris looks odd in front of Number 10. I know we're inevitably going to be dealing in different shades of mediocrity, but is it too much to ask to have a leader who doesn't move like someone who's wet themselves on an electric blanket? Like a horny pile of laundry, or a cross between Winston Churchill and carbon monoxide, he won a majority partly because his illegitimate children now constitute a considerable voting bloc. Of course he hates burkas: he might accidentally chat up someone he's already impregnated. Becoming Tory leader is hard. You need both a unifying acceptance speech and the stomach for the inauguration ceremony, where you must precision-urinate into a box of soil from Robin Hood's grave while a faceless shadow plays 'Jerusalem' backwards on a banjo fashioned from Margaret Thatcher's tibia. The process has bred a leader immune to humiliation; a man who would still have the blank eyes of a dead snake if he was instructed to fart the national anthem on a Japanese game show.

I'm convinced that reactionary politics consciously or unconsciously offers up outliers to make the people it invests with power seem almost normal. When you're looking for distraction in these dumbed-down times, where seeing tragedy on a West End stage probably means going to a Bee Gees musical, something very basic might be required. Step forward Jacob Rees-Mogg, a composite figure drawn from the nightmares of eighteenth-century child millworkers. He looks like a *Punch* cartoon of the first giraffe in England, and maintains the general air of someone who's had a wank to the Book of Deuteronomy. Rees-Mogg, a one-man generation gap, could perhaps best serve mankind by posing in speedos for an effigy to nail above our doors that's sufficiently powerful to scare off a marauding virus. It's hard to call people like this an anachronism when in many ways they are the perfect people to stand in a baroque debating chamber engaged in formalised debate over a golden mace. Perhaps it is we who are fooling ourselves, thinking that things have moved on, when the political settlement in this country isn't so very different from the 1920s.

Perhaps we are in an advanced stage of transitioning into a managed democracy, and an increasingly disengaged and atomised public are being asked to take part in an affirmatory rather than participatory politics. Despite looking like someone inflated Andy Warhol's corpse, Johnson is in many ways the perfect front man for this – he looks incapable of carrying out real politics, and seeing him talk about a fiscal stimulus package or whatever is like watching a racoon giving a TED talk. Indeed, after an American trade deal is completed, there's a good chance we can look forward to an actual cessation of our politics, much of it replaced with investor-state resolution. Perhaps we need a new post-Brexit logo: I'd suggest 'Britain is open for business' above Union Jack knickers round a pair of ankles.

So what will this government actually do? They will no doubt steer towards some kind of social conservatism, but its effects will be limited, for white people at least. Tories are committed to keeping marriages together, admittedly by a combination of keeping people out at work so long that they barely meet, and negative equity. The thought of something truly reactionary like bringing back hanging is quaintly optimistic about where crime and justice is right now. To actually get arrested; for there to be enough staff to process your case and write it all down once Yvonne comes back with the pencil; to be found guilty despite the person you killed owning a moped, or living near an estate, or having read *Fifty Shades of Grey* a couple of times; to remain in prison long enough to not incur an overdue charge on your library book; and for budgets to stretch to an executioner, some gallows and strong rope, rather than just chucking you the belt they took off the one person to be arrested in a suit this decade. To get past all that to actually get hanged would be an achievement close to completing *Dark Souls III* on Quaaludes. Of course, it's odd that it's always people who vote for a Tory government that want capital punishment – I mean, you don't really need both.

Some profoundly depressing attitudes will no doubt be entrenched under this parliament. General law and order theory now seems to be that if you're black you'll commit crime, if you're white you won't: fourteen-year-old black kid stabbed in the street in broad daylight – 'shouldn't have been driving a moped'; twenty-five-year-old white guy chokes a girl to death while watching porn – 'look, we have so few pleasures these days...' I blame texting: in the old days Tories would murmur that white-collar crime shouldn't count, and then one day I suppose 'collar' just took up too many characters. There will be some profoundly illiberal developments that will focus on scapegoating minorities. As with Windrush, much of it will involve structural racism that blames victims for the failings of the state. For example, no funding for terrorists to be de-radicalised makes us culpable as a society for their actions on release. The only way they're currently being integrated into society is by blasting their brain tissue permanently into the hinge of a Sainsbury's Local.

There will also be policies aimed as a nod towards the

kind of social conservatism that the government wishes to encourage. One such idea that has already been floated is cheap rail travel for UK military veterans. Good. It means they'll be able to stalk the partner who left them because they scream every time they blink and see their best friend's legs boomerang round a poppy field. I'm all for discounted rail travel for veterans. If only as it might bring some much-needed discipline to the quiet carriage; maybe a kid would be less keen to pull out that plastic trumpet if they knew in a nearby seat could be a trained killer wrestling with PTSD. I worry about unintended consequences. UK rail travel's now so pricey a discount for serving could provide a powerful recruitment incentive. The last thing an Afghan farmer needs to hear before he's perforated is a tearfully whimpered, 'I'm sorry, it's only so I can afford a Bletchley to Euston season ticket.'

I'd imagine gerrymandering will be a key theme of this parliament. Soon the government will introduce measures where you'll only be allowed to vote if you can produce a passport or driving licence – presumably because people are more likely to vote for another Tory government if they have the option of fleeing the society they create. Proposed voter ID laws are forecast to deny up to three million people, largely from marginalised groups, the right to vote. On the other hand, the government might find this kind of electoral boost so attractive that they decide against microchipping us, so swings and roundabouts. Rather than ID, I think your right to vote should be decided by playing the theme to *Michael McIntyre's Big Show* and seeing if you hum along. Voting will be done by algorithm – whoever you clicked on most that year will be PM. To be honest I think a cabinet run by cats and someone skateboarding off a staircase will at least put more funding into comfortable public spaces. Of course, if governments were really populist they'd be run by the highest watched on Pornhub. To be fair, the ability to take it up the arse gleefully both helps in trade negotiations and brings us back to the original intent of democracy, which was basically to elevate normal blokes so they could get blue-tick bum sex as well.

I predict proportional representation will continue to be a non-issue, and it's a shame. Clearly democracy isn't a perfect system, in a country where we put instructions on shampoo, but we have persisted with a patently unfair voting system where a minority of the electorate can provide a government with an overwhelming mandate. We are a people that seems to attach importance to things happening decisively, even when we largely disagree with them. It's remarkable how much a post-colonial society's attitudes overlap with those of the Mafia.

Naturally, the creeping privatisation of the NHS will continue. Just some harmless private involvement to provide little frills to those who can afford it. I confess I recently paid quite a bit extra to have the doctor examine my prostate using the exact same gloves worn by Audrey Hepburn in *Breakfast at Tiffany's* (diamonds may well be a girl's best friend, but believe me they're not a large intestine's). Another fairly safe bet is that with a lowering of environmental standards we can expect businesses to be pumping a lot more pollution into our rivers. Which you may brush off, thinking it doesn't affect you, but remember those rivers will be flowing through your front room every winter, until in twenty years they completely dry up. My advice is to try to move to a river that's near a factory that disposes of the chemicals they use to clean carpets and upholstery, so you can get a head start on the spring clean.

There will no doubt be the odd policy to keep the North on side: reducing the number of street homeless by reopening the odd library, or perhaps a little boost to morale for the Midlands by announcing plans to curtain off Dudley. Indeed, government investment is currently so low, it would be hard not to make it seem like it had increased. But this will all have to compete with the government's stated plan to redirect council funding from the areas that house these newly won seats to Tory shires. Another thing worth noting is that

Britain is a country where lack of investment has historically been offset by cheap imported labour – how can this be squared with the government's rhetoric on limiting migration? Johnson's administration knows what it has to do to shore itself up electorally, but its inherent conflicts may make this difficult in practice.

There are other economic reasons to think that it will be difficult for the Conservatives to form as broad an electoral coalition next time round. We are at the end of a cycle of financialisation, where governments privatised industries and funded public projects through PFI, possibly because we're a society where more overt bribery is frowned upon. Where even the family became financialised, as wage growth was replaced by debt. No British person would dream of telling you their net worth, but the national pastime is buying a house that allows you to guess. In previous generations the Conservatives hoped that young people would become more conservative as they got mortgages, or advanced up the career ladder, or something else that none of them will ever do again. But I don't know that this government will really care about that: to many Tories the generation gap means little more than the distance separating them on their reverse stroke from a teenage prostitute.

I always think that demographic-based optimism from the left tends to be slightly overstated, especially as old people are living longer. Possibly down to medical advances, or possibly from spite. Property certainly looks bad for the next generation. Though if the government continues with its current housing policies, soon moving home will be as easy as just dragging a papier-mâché shell into a different postcode. We'll just have to embrace the new realities like job sharing: you'll do your job up till later this year, then someone in the Far East will do it. Self-employed may mean no pension, sick or holiday pay but you are Your. Own. Boss! Have to get down to Tesco for when they put on the yellow stickers? Who do you need permission from? That's right... YOU! You're the BOSS!'

Dominic Cummings (his surname comes from the Middle English word for the wet patch) is someone Johnson believes to be the source of inspiring ideas because his head is shaped like a light bulb. I'm not comfortable with the Tories being so in thrall to an unelected adviser: it hardly seems fair on the corporate lobbyists. Dominic Cummings is someone who believes that with the right mindset you can achieve anything apart from properly funded social care. Perhaps the gig economy can help out with social care, so that anyone with a bike can underbid to spend the day squirting soup through a pensioner's letterbox; and how silly that police armed response teams still take out lethal suspects, when, once cornered, the shot could be sold to an American safari tourist.

Perhaps Cummings has been sent to test the resolve of humanity... a creature that's existed since the dawn of time to thwart human potential, his likeness glimpsed in the margins of cave paintings, hieroglyphs and woodcuts. His voice first heard in ancient Mesopotamia, whispering very faintly in the breeze when the crops failed: 'That'll be down to those fucking Sumerians... merians... erians... rians.' Tutankhamun's PR guy perhaps – 'Believe me, your highness, they'll be too distracted to notice your grain tax if you just strap on this giant chin.' Maybe he's not real in the conventional sense, but a creature brought into being by mass telepathy when a nation attains a sufficient level of self-loathing; so that if we learn to love, live and care, he will shrink. A year of a kinder Britain may reduce him to fending off spiders with a hat pin.

Whatever happens with Brexit, Cummings will ensure that deregulation will be a key theme of this parliament. Soon the only red tape in this country will be across the finish line of the compulsory Food Bank Olympics – victors wheezing onto the podium, only to spend the national anthem scratching at the medal to try and get the foil off the chocolate. Letting people sell their labour at any price will liberate them from the tyranny of the nanny state: taking evening classes in yoga in the hope that you can pick up work as a coffee table; a satnav now beyond your reach, you're reduced to finding your way back to your hovel with only the aid of a parrot crossbred with a homing pigeon.

This government's instincts will be technocratic, although this will be downplayed, because it sounds far too European. As the Conservatives try to sandbag their gains in the north and Midlands of England, we might expect some limited attempts to address inequality because marginal voters are now lower down the income scale. This will probably take the form of borrowing to fund infrastructure projects in those areas, because Dominic Cummings, from what we can tell, isn't ideologically opposed to economic intervention, and Boris Johnson barely has an ideology. Naturally this will be fuelled by opportunism rather than empathy. With Dom on the tiller it'll be all about incorporating private sector know-how. 'Direct cash payments for single mothers? Sounds like a job for the guys at Spearmint Rhino!' How can Boris understand hardship? The only time he's ever truly suffered was back at Eton when, after getting caught whistling after lights out, he was forced to use his genitalia as a rudimentary toasting fork.

I'm probably more optimistic about the future of left politics in Britain than recent evidence would suggest is rational. Remember that in 2005 the Tories won just 198 seats, yet by the next election they'll have been in government for fourteen years. Indeed, I think anyone who promises free earphones to people watching loud samba videos on the bus might sweep to power. But the left has so far been unable to use the increasing politicisation of society to any real advantage. The things that the Labour Party assumes – some kind of homogeneity by area; a form of class consciousness, however weak; even some kind of belief that political change is possible – have all been severely eroded. Corbyn's dream of funding social care is as dead as a pensioner who's failed to reach their doorknob after sliding down an avalanche of junk mail. Crippling care costs will soon even be reflected in our eulogies: 'Ethel was a fighter, but eventually we managed to screw the lid down.'

Labour's 2019 trigger ballots saw no MPs deselected, which suggests a lack of appetite for purges and a membership that has radical policy instincts without radical political instincts. The party has its work cut out because recently it always seems to be fighting on two fronts. Not just against itself, but also against people who might be considering joining it. I always got an extraordinary amount of hatred from Corbyn supporters, and a part of it is that Labour activists are still largely drawn from the bandwidth of classes that expect my job to be performed by a public school, Oxbridge-educated Englishman. Class awareness is pervasive in Britain, and I suppose it's inevitable that satirists from a working-class Scottish background are greeted with the kind of low-key alarm normally reserved for a cockney gynaecologist.

Labour's online supporters seem to have adopted an unusual strategy of reaching out to people who already agree with them and telling them to fuck off. I don't want to over-state things here: it wasn't a big factor in the election, and there is an obvious contradiction in expecting to see mass movements operate within narrow acceptable boundaries of behaviour. Yet, online at least, the co-morbidity of post-colo-nial entitlement meeting male narcissism, and vanguardism, has developed into a potent brew for demotivating potential allies. Left-wingers aren't uniquely unpleasant online, but their unpleasantness is uniquely off-brand. I sometimes won-der if the change needed on the British left may be one that is entirely incompatible with the post-colonial mindset: the realisation that it's your own consciousness that you have to raise. Traditionally, when the psychedelic writers talk about raising consciousness, it contains the idea of understanding our personal insignificance and escaping the ego. In some ways this echoes Marxist writers' themes of raising class-con-sciousness; understanding the strength of the collective rather than the individual. The Labour left's ecosystem of Twitter spats and purity tests would seem to be entirely anti-pathetic to such advances. I often think that the trouble with self-identifying as a good person in a society like ours is that you're subject to the same forces as everybody else; you're just less aware of them.

One problem on the left that may stem from the amount of time they spend online is that sometimes they have an attachment to ideas that sound good but don't really play out that well if you think about them. 'Speak Truth to Power' has become a popular goal over the last decade or so. It's an old Quaker term that was popularised during their resistance to the Vietnam War. I think it has literally become axiomatic because it sounds quite good when you say it. What would be the point of me Speaking Truth to Boris Johnson? He would simply give me an amused look that simultaneously said, 'You don't know the half of it, mate,' and, 'How did you get past my security?'

Of course, reactionary 'anti-woke' types are operating in ignorance at best, and often in bad faith. Their basic position is 'some people are so marginalised that they have to build a language to describe their oppression, but the real victim is me, who has to learn a new word every nine months'. Yet I think when it comes to culture the left is often guilty of muddy thinking, and a poor choice of targets. I know that it's frustrating that some actor complains about the (histori-cally accurate) casting of Sikh soldiers in a First World War movie (from the culture that brought you white Jesus this is admittedly galling), but there are things that matter more and it would be better to concentrate on them. At the time of writing the British left seems to have no real view on who should be the next Director-General of the BBC. It's worth noting that the aspect of the BBC's news structure that is most damaging to Labour – that the BBC tends to take its agenda from the press, who take theirs from Westminster briefings – is apparently too nuanced a point to be addressed by the Labour left, and it is almost never mentioned.

Things will be very different in ten years' time if the BBC loses its licence fee funding. The Corporation will be stripped back and sold off until all news, sport and comment will be created and broadcast by Laura Kuenssberg. She will be the last physical remnant of the BBC. Roaming from town to town like an itinerant knife sharpener. With the familiar cry of, 'I'm Laura Kuenssberg. I AM the BBC and I AM the news. But before the headlines, let's have a look at the weather in your area.' It's during this brief moment, where the gathered crowd tip their heads towards the heavens to look at the weather in their area, that Laura slips off her boots and pops on a pair of kitten heels. Shakes the road dust from her jacket. Spits onto her hand and cleans her face before she's ready to uphold the values of the BBC. To inform, to educate and to entertain. She begins by informing. There are still pockets of humanity in the south and the far north, but she fears everything south of Carlisle and north of Manchester has perished.

She adds further details, that a nearby village has recently burned to the ground during an accident at the annual cheese-rolling festival. It's a tale she tells every village, but hearing the misfortunes of their local rivals perks up the crowd and gives Laura a better chance of collecting more bread and dried meats when she passes round her hat at the end. Harking back to the glory days of the BBC, she might then shout some advice to a hag about how she might want to fix up her garden. 'Put more flowers in it, and trees. I understand it serves its purpose as a boneyard, but that doesn't mean you couldn't pop a few daisies in there.' And then a recipe for old times' sake. 'Make soup,' she suggests. To be fair politics were more her thing, but as the only remaining tangible expression of the BBC, she tries. As the crowd disperses, Laura again considers switching to ITV, who have offered her a mule and some firelighters.

But what sort of future is there for the Labour Party? Keir Starmer is a man with the stage presence of the Higgs boson, whose dating profile would simply read 'alive'. He seems to be viewed as electable by Labour members largely because he looks like someone playing a prime minister in an old Spice Girls' video. He will certainly provide a strong opposition to satire: he is difficult to joke about, in the same way that it is difficult to write jokes about brown wrapping paper or the frozen tundra. I predict that the new Labour leader will find it difficult to make any early impact. The endless internal election will have robbed him of any novelty value; Boris will reduce the vocabulary of politics to that of a Channel 5 football pundit who's spent a week in a holiday cottage with low doorways; and the Conservatives will find it relatively easy to present Starmer, to a lot of voters, as one of the pen-pushers who ruin their lives.

Ironically for a Brexit election, we seem to have chosen to accept that decisions affecting our lives are largely incapable of being influenced. Of course, technology can make politicians seem closer. Smartphones, Twitter, telescopic sights – yet, paradoxically, it has actually rendered them as distant and symbolic as Pokémon. In this sense, Keir Starmer is a good candidate to provide a different kind of unreality from Johnson. The smooth managerial sense of politics occurring elsewhere, rather than the experience of watching a clown have a heart attack while being dimly aware of an explosion in the distance.

For many reasons, I think the difficulty of Labour being able to form a minority government at the next election is overstated. Yes, it's statistically improbable, but their electoral coalition will no longer be divided by Brexit. Keir Starmer will provide an Establishment face for another opportunity for our dying order of things to replicate itself – this time without any of the resources of Empire, or the support of the EU – on a burning world.

The British left online seems to see trending on Twitter as an end in itself. Really, you can only be politically active online in the same way you can be sexually active online, and the far right sees all its online activities as staging posts to recruitment. Yet in some ways the left have dealt with the far right better than the mainstream media. They are correct to refuse to debate and platform these goons; we already know what their case is. Personally, I think we had quite a thorough debate about the whole thing in the 1940s. Is there some broader point they were getting to that the Allies interrupted? I think the perfect plot for a satire would be a group of young white men posting racism and misogyny for a laugh, and gradually finding that, because of the structural prejudices of their society, they were all really into it. Sadly, it has been scuppered by the alt-right doing it in real life.

Good old Tommy Robinson, always smiling, like a golliwog in negative. Of course, Tommy Robinson isn't even his real name; his real name sounds like his fake name's probation officer. He chose a name that sounds like a character in a war comic, the sort of loveable, machine-gun-toting Second World War British squaddie who would have seen it as his duty to kill this Tommy Robinson. Since being born on a sunbed, this furious boiled potato has nurtured Britain's sense of racial grievance with the patience and care you only see in someone who truly believes that they can monetise it.

Tommy Robinson is evidence of the horror that can result when a social inadequate hasn't the mental capacity to just learn a few magic tricks. At first I clung to the most plausible explanation – he was just a Turner Prize entry that had gone rogue. Of course, far-right views have long been normalised, certainly in comparison to far-left ones. You rarely hear anyone complaining that their taxi driver wouldn't stop going on about Gramsci, or see folk getting banned from football grounds for Marxist chanting. Which is fair enough; it's tricky getting 'purge the counter-revolutionaries for bourgeois deviation!' to sync up with a vuvuzela. Obviously, there's more hatred on the hard right, but they do seem to have mastered something the left seems to find so hard – directing it outwards.

One of the tragedies of the far right's resurgence is that I am considered a moderate now. The last time there were this many people to the right of me I was being picked for sports. The far right in Britain are using social media to recruit while the left use it to berate people for liking problematic music videos. I think a problem for the left is their essentialism: they see people as either good or bad, and the role of activism focuses on energising the good ones. The right's more effective philosophy is that both sides are fighting over the same potential voters and members, and people co-opted into the far right are often from groups socialists feel are their natural constituencies. There was a prototype version of Tommy Robinson, Britain First's Paul Golding, who seemed to concentrate on shouting at kebab shops. The next version might be something we really have to worry about. The next version will have even more exposure, and elite support, because late-stage capitalism generally prefers fascism to equality.

Perhaps much of the modern British political landscape represents the natural endpoint of individualism. With a philosophy where people are told that it is their sense of self that is important, why wouldn't they distrust experts, why wouldn't they look inside themselves for guidance? When we look inside ourselves we tend to find not ideologies but neuroses. Many people in Britain lately seem to have looked into their hearts and found little more than a dislike of hearing a conversation in another language, a hatred of women and a gnawing fear that they're being taken for a mug.

One thing that's useful to remember when trying to understand British politics is that for even the politically engaged English person it seems to require an act of will to remember that Scotland, Wales, and particularly Northern Ireland, exist. For those countries, it can be a little like being locked in the basement of someone who doesn't fancy you anymore. In England, for Conservatives and Labour alike, an instinctive rejection of independent nationalism is part of the imperial hangover. This is so pronounced that broad elements of Labour will often fret over how to re-engage with the sort of nationalism that doesn't like immigrants, while maintaining that the Scottish ones that want a bit more investment in public services are an evil too great to even acknowledge.

Let's return to the theme we started with and take another look at colonial history: this time Scotland's. There are lots of things that Scottish people don't generally know about their own history. For example, most Scots don't know that the Forth river is so named because water is the fourth most popular liquid in Scotland. That the Scottish New Year tradition of receiving a 'first foot' originally involved being pleasured by a man with immense genitalia. Or that there used to be a Scottish donor card, which read, 'After my death I'd like my liver to be put in a jar and used in cautionary school assemblies about lifestyle choices, or for jump-starting a barbecue.' Scotland's union with England is another thing that's often viewed quite simplistically. The Act of Union sounds a bit like a sexual euphemism, and, as with many a loveless coupling, oil really helps. The Union was a deal between the ruling classes, and the majority of the Scottish population was ignored, setting a tone that has been adopted by Westminster to this day.

The Union was about a lot of things. One that's rarely mentioned is the need for imperial manpower: England needed more bodies to serve in its armies. Although it wasn't immediately obvious how they could increase their population by aligning with a country which was, at that point in history, burning anyone with a womb and a cat. After years of negotiation the Act of Union came into effect on 1 May 1707, and immediately riots began in Edinburgh. What could have persuaded Scottish nobles to hand over their power to Westminster and dissolve the Scottish parliament? A small matter of the sum of £398,000, an amount that was equal to the loss of something called the Darien scheme.

In 1695 there had begun a period of famine and disease in Scotland which became known as the 'Seven Ill Years'. Life expectancy in Scotland at this time was around eight. People would get married at three, have a family at five and retire at seven. If you lived until ten you were considered a witch and drowned. I'm joking, of course: you were cooked and eaten. Starvation claimed the lives of between 5 and 15 per cent of the population. In Aberdeenshire, a quarter of the population died. It's impossible to imagine today what the sense of despair in Aberdeen in the 1690s would have been like without going to Inverness today.

Scotland wanted to be a mercantile power. But we'd just spent seven years in famine. What exactly were we hoping to trade? Here's a drawing of a loaf. Who wants to give me sapphires and rubies in exchange for my memories of a potato? These were desperate times, but sometimes even in the bleakest situation someone can have an idea that can make everything just that little bit worse. The idea was that Scotland should start its own colony in Panama. I won't say nothing came of the Darien scheme. Its terrible failure in Latin America did provide a handy blueprint for Scotland's 1978 World Cup. The scheme failed because of one single but crucial flaw: it was completely shit. Scots thinking they could thrive in equatorial heat shows the same level of optimism as Joan of Arc rubbing on some Factor 20.

Scottish investors raised £400,000 for the scheme, which was an extraordinary amount of money in those days. The area in Panama the Scots chose to colonise is still virtually uninhabitable today and is twinned with Dunfermline. After just eight months, in July 1699 the colony was abandoned. Only 300 of the 1,200 settlers survived. By the time it was abandoned, a second expedition of a thousand colonists had already set off. They were somewhat luckier in that they died more quickly. Scottish nobles were bankrupted by the Darien scheme and this was one of the major motivators of the 1707 Act of Union. About a fifth of Scotland's entire wealth had been sunk into the scheme and lost. Scotland had little choice but to hitch its wrecked fortunes to the yoke of England.

Scottish national identity, the idea of Scotland as a unified nation, rather than an uneasy collection of Highlanders and Lowlanders, post-dates the Union. To some extent it was consciously created, with Sir Walter Scott being a key figure in imagining it into existence. As the academic Neil Davidson argues, there hasn't really been a Scottish identity separate from the Union. The corollary of this is that the modern English identity is a British identity. For this reason, this Conservative government will never grant another referendum, not just because they can't imagine themselves as half an island in the middle of nowhere, without any idea about where to park their nukes, but because they have literally no understanding of themselves outside of the Union. In the reactionary mind, Scottish people living lives stunted of opportunity, often in poverty, is an acceptable price to pay to fulfil an ideology. I don't know that Labour's position – that Scottish people should live in those conditions in the hope that they might kick half a dozen extra seats their way occasionally – is really ethically much better.

When you understand the colonial history, it seems obvious that the SNP, a kind of political wing of the Scottish managerial class, sees independence as the forging of a

Scottish version of the British state. Indeed, the 2014 campaign sought to keep not just the monarch, but the pound. They would certainly never call their own referendum. An illegal referendum held in Scotland would not be recognised or respected by Westminster, making it no different from anything else that happens in Scotland. Personally, I quite like the idea of an illegal referendum: perhaps you can only get your ballot paper by contacting a guy on Facebook Marketplace and then meeting him after dark in an Asda car park.

As you've probably gathered, I don't really know what the future holds for Britain, or even for me. I write in my local park any days that the Scottish weather allows, and I always start by checking my Instagram DMs for the addicts – almost always alcoholics – who contact me there. There is a certain type of drinker who finds it very difficult to go to their first meeting, or consider therapy. I've thought of some tricks for getting yourself to do this, and I try to help everyone who writes. In fact, I sometimes think that this is what I really do now: directly touching the dozen or so people a year who get into recovery is surely bigger than any effect my work has. You have no idea how silly it feels to even type 'my work' when you're a comedian. Today as I went through this little ritual, it occurred to me that something has been lost here.

When your nihilists are reduced to altruism, it's probably a bad sign. We had a purpose once in society. We were a dark lens: the people who persuaded you to move away from the poisoned stream. We were also the sort of self-regarding pricks who called ourselves a dark lens, and were generally not great at parties. Now, I suppose, things are too desperate for that – all the streams are poisoned, and there's nowhere to move to – and we find ourselves pulling an oar alongside sociologists, community activists and charity workers: all the well-meaning, decent people who in happier times we could have berated and travestied. But as we're all here now, I'll tell you what I tell the people in my DMs: that despair is really a failure of perspective. Despair is a moment that pretends to be permanent. There are good reasons to be hopeful; there is a place beyond this moment, and we can, if we choose to, get up off our knees and go there together.

AFTERWORD

In 1924, inspired by a sensational essay they had published the previous year, the publishers Kegan Paul launched a series of small, elegant books called To-Day and To-Morrow. The founding essay was *Daedalus; or, Science and the Future*, and its author, the biologist J. B. S. Haldane, made several striking predictions: genetic modification, wind power, artificial food. But the idea that captured the imagination of his contemporaries was what he called 'ectogenesis' – the gestation of embryos in artificial wombs. Haldane's friend Aldous Huxley included it in his novel *Brave New World*, in which humans are cloned and mass-produced in 'Hatcheries' (it was Haldane who later gave us the word 'clone'). Fast-forward almost a century, and scientists have now trialled ectogenesis on sheep and are exploring its potential for saving dangerously premature babies.

Haldane took no prisoners as he hurtled through the ages and all the major sciences, weighing up what was still to be done. Perhaps because it was his discipline, he was convinced that the next exciting scientific discoveries would be made not in physics but in biology. So, his Daedalus is not the familiar pioneer of flight but the first genetic engineer – the designer of the contraption that enabled King Minos's wife to mate with a bull and produce the Minotaur. Predictions have an unstable afterlife; their truth changes with the world, and while Haldane was brilliant on – and made a major contribution to – genetics, he was sceptical about the possibility of nuclear power. In the wake of the Second World War, and the realities of atom bombs, hydrogen bombs and nuclear power stations, his view of the sciences appeared wide of the mark. Later, when the Human Genome Project became news, he emerged as a prophet again. But while biotech certainly still preoccupies us two decades on, it is the computer that we see ushering in the definitive transformations of the age: artificial intelligence, machine learning, blockchain. And, remarkably, the computer is the one major modern development that not only Haldane but all the To-Day and To-Morrow writers missed.

By 1931, when the series was wound up, it ran to 110 books. They covered many of the subjects that mattered most at the time, from the future of marriage to the future of war, the future of art to the future of the British Empire. Most of To-Day and To-morrow's contributors were progressive, rationalist and intelligent, in favour of a World State and sceptical of eugenics. They wrote well, and were sometimes very funny, and the essays on the future of clothes and the future of nonsense in particular are wonderfully eccentric. And, of course, Haldane wasn't the only visionary. Many of the other writers contributed equally far-sighted ideas: Dora Russell suggested something akin to universal basic income for mothers; J. D. Bernal imagined wirelessly networked cyborgs – a cross between social media and the Internet of things; while Vera Brittain waxed confident about the enshrinement of women's rights in law.

What really stands out now is how, on the whole, the authors seemed to feel freer to be imaginative about the future than our contemporaries tend to be when they make predictions. There seems to be something about the long-form essay that freed the To-Day and To-morrow authors to see further ahead than a short journalistic piece could. Pursuing the logic of an individual vision, while also responding to what others projected, led them to dive deep into their topics in ways that are hard for the more tightly collaborative think-tank approaches of today to replicate. They were also more constructive than most of our contemporary future-thinkers. Of course we'd be mad not to worry about the climate crisis, the mass displacement of people(s), the risks of AI, new diseases (I'm writing this at the height – *maybe* – of COVID-19), asteroid collision and other apocalyptic scenarios. But if we're not only to survive these but also to thrive, we need to think beyond them as well as about them.

We are now almost a century on from the launch of To-Day and Tomorrow, and it feels like the right time to try this thought experiment again. So, for this first set of FUTURES, we have assembled a diverse group of brilliant writers with provocative ideas and visions. The point is not so much to prophesy as to generate new ideas about possibilities that could help us realise a future we might want to inhabit. To-Day and To-Morrow launched visions that helped create the modern world. The challenges we face now are, obviously, different from those of the 1920s and 30s. But our aspirations for FUTURES are the same. We want to change the conversation about what lies ahead so we can better imagine, understand and articulate the new worlds we might want to create.

Professor Max Saunders, March 2020

Max Saunders's Imagined Futures: Writing, Science, and Modernity in the To-Day and To-Morrow Book Series, 1923–31 *was published by Oxford University Press in 2019.*

Unbound is the world's first crowdfunding publisher, established in 2011.

We believe that wonderful things can happen when you clear a path for people who share a passion. That's why we've built a platform that brings together readers and authors to crowdfund books they believe in – and give fresh ideas that don't fit the traditional mould the chance they deserve.

This book is in your hands because readers made it possible. Everyone who pledged their support is listed below. Join them by visiting unbound.com and supporting a book today.

With special thanks to Jo Greenslade and Ark Schools

Caspar Addyman	Sarah Bennett	John Boxall
Kathy Allen	James Benussi	Zara Bredin
John Attridge	Steve Bindley	Catherine Breslin
William Ayles	Kate Bird	Fabia Bromovsky
Stuart Banks	Ian Blatchford	Victoria Bryant
David Barker	Su Bonfanti	Nicki Burns
Stephen Beagrie	Ed Bonnell	Paul David Burns
Ghassan Bejjani	Stuart Bowdler	Imogen Butler

Steve Byrne
Bob Callard
Ella Cape-Davenhill
NJ Cesar
Neil Chavner
Brendan Clarke
Nick Clarke
Peter Clasen
Jane Clifford
Fiona Clifft
Rhonda Cole
David-John Collins
Robert Collins
Alexander Colmer
Laura Colombino
Joseph Cordery
Andrew Correia
Peter Cosgrove
Nicola Crowell
Paolo Cuomo
Mary Curnock
   Cook
Matthew d'Ancona
Tom Daly
Eileen Davidson

Joshua Davies
Edmund Davison
Victoria Davison
Sarah Denton
Jeremy Dicker
Lewis Dimmick
Kevin Donnellon
Linda Edge
Helen Edwards
Michael Elliott
Dominic Emery
Nic Fallows
Joanna Flood
Graham Folmer
Cedric Fontanille
Robert Forsyth
Oliver Francis
D Franklin
The FUTURES
   team
Josh Gaillemin
Brian Gee
Lisa Gee
Sarah Gee
Charley Gilbert

Tom Gillingwater
Jordan Goble
George Goodfellow
John Gordon
Molly Gordon
Paul Gould
Brice Goureau
Melanie Gow
Keith Grady
Marlies Gration
Jon Gray
Scott Greenwell
Georgia Greer
John Grout
Steve Grycuk
Nicola Haggett
Greg Halfacre
Elizabeth Hall
Skye Hallam
Chloe Hardy
Nicola Harford
Richard Harvey
Nick Helweg-
   Larsen
Paul Higgins

Gemma Hitchens

Maggie Hobbs

Meaghan Hook

Simon Howard

Nick Hubble

Simon Huggins

Jenny Hynd

Maggie Jack

Andy Johnson

Rebecca Jones

Danny Josephs

Tanu Kaskinen

Matthew Keegan

Christopher Kelly

Hilary Kemp

Luke Kemp

Fraser Kerr

Adam Khan

Dan Kieran

Andrew Knight

Christine Knight-
    Maunder

Lauren Knussen

Florian Kogler

Michael Kowalski

Simon Krystman

Nikki Land

Ben Lappin

Lyndsey Lawrence

Benedict Leigh

Fiona Lensvelt

Max Lensvelt

Sonny Leong

Miriam Levitin

Joanne Limburg

Linds

Valerie Lindsay

Ivan Lowe

Brian Lunn

Nicola Lynch

Rob MacAndrew

Andrew
    MacGarvey

Jem Mackay

Innes Macleod

Lewis MacRae

Paul Martin

Chris Matthias

Jenny McCullough

Michael McDowall

John McGowan

Neil McLaren

Adrian Melrose

John Mitchinson

Ronald Mitchinson

Kyna Morgan

Ian Morley

Tony Mulvahil

Robin Mulvihill

Peter Mummery

Tessa Murray

Janet Musgrove

James Nash

Carlo Navato

Kelvin Nel

John New

Sorcha Ní
    Mhaonaigh

Christopher Norris

Tim O'Connor

Mark O'Neill

Brian Padley

Michael Paley

Euan Palmer

Nic Parsons

Jaynesh Patel

Don Paterson

Sumit Paul-
  Choudhury

Matthew Pearson

Pauline Peirce

Nick Petre

Benjamin Poliak

Justin Pollard

Harriet Posner

Samantha Potter

Mark Poulson

Kate Pullinger

Slam Raman

Padraig Reade

Colette Reap

Suzanne Reynolds

John Rice Doyle

Stephen Ross

Charlotte Rump

Stuart Rutherford

Keith Ruttle

Cassedy Ryan

Ruth Sacks

Luke Sanders

Martin Saugnac

Max Saunders

Eleanor Scharer

Daniel
  Schwickerath

Duncan Scovil

Alexander Sehmer

Rossa Shanks

Gillian Shearn

Paul Skinner

Christopher Smith

Jan Smith

Katie Smith

Matthew Spicer

Paul Squires

Wendy Staden

Nicola Stanhope

Keith Stewart

Freddie Stockler

Nick Stringer

Elizabeth Suffling

Gilane Tawadros

Georgette Taylor

Richard Taylor

Bronwen Thomas

Luke Thornton

Lydia Titterington

Sophie Truepenny

Mark Turner

Geoff Underwood

Maarten van den
  Belt

Suzan Vanneck

Danielle Vides

Emma Visick

Gabriel Vogt

Claire Walker

Sir Harold Walker

Suzi Watford

Richard White

John Williams

Ross Williams

Catherine
  Williamson

Philip Wilson

Luke Young

Angelique &
  Stefano Zuppet